Ten Poe
about Rc

ex libris

Candlestick Press

Published by:
Candlestick Press,
Diversity House, 72 Nottingham Road, Arnold, Nottingham UK NG5 6LF
www.candlestickpress.co.uk

Design and typesetting by Diversity Creative Marketing Solutions Ltd.,
www.diversity.agency

Printed by Ratcliff & Roper Print Group, Nottinghamshire, UK

Selection and Introduction © Hamish Whyte, 2018

Cover illustration © Sam Cannon, 2018
www.samcannonart.co.uk

Candlestick Press monogram © Barbara Shaw, 2008

© Candlestick Press, 2018
Reprinted 2019, 2021

ISBN 978 1 907598 75 3

Acknowledgements:

The poems in this pamphlet are reprinted from the following books, all by
permission of the publishers listed unless stated otherwise. Every effort has
been made to trace the copyright holders of the poems published in this book.
The editor and publisher apologise if any material has been included without
permission or without the appropriate acknowledgement, and would be glad to be
told of anyone who has not been consulted.

Thanks are due to all the copyright holders cited below for their kind permission:

Fleur Adcock, *Dragon Talk* (Bloodaxe Books, 2009) www.bloodaxebooks.com

UA Fanthorpe, *Christmas Poems* (Enitharmon Press, 2002)

John Freeman, *What Possessed Me* (Worple Press, Tonbridge, 2016) by kind
permission of the author

Stanley Kunitz, "Robin Redbreast". Copyright © 1969 by Stanley Kunitz,
Passing Through: The Later Poems, New and Selected. Used by permission of W.
W. Norton & Company, Inc. (W. W. Norton & Co., 1997)

Norman MacCaig, *The Poems of Norman MacCaig* (Birlinn; Polygon, 2007)

Peter Walton, *The Cheerfulness of Sparrows* (Shoestring Press, 1997)

Hamish Whyte, *Window on the Garden* (Botanic Press & Essence Press, 2006) by
permission of the author

Where poets are no longer living, their dates are given.

All permissions cleared courtesy of Swift Permissions
(swiftpermissions@gmail.com)

Contents

Introduction

The robin is Britain's favourite bird. It's hard not to love
the robin, the jolly dash of red, cheeky eye, friendliness to
humans. It has proved irresistible to writers too, from Anon to
Wordsworth. Attractive birds, they're notoriously aggressive, but
in fact seldom indulge in combat.

Robins are most associated with winter and have become a
staple image on Christmas cards. Why this should be has never
been satisfactorily explained – possibly their red breast suggests
an echo of holly berries and there are stories about robins and
Jesus (there was one in the stable, apparently). UA Fanthorpe,
Norman MacCaig and Peter Walton deal with this aspect in their
own light but serious ways. Robins are not of course just for
Christmas. They sing the whole of the year, John Clare noted.
They are constant garden visitors. They know humans provide
extra sustenance, as in Fleur Adcock's poem.

There are perhaps no 'great' poems about robins – robins are too
familiar, but maybe that's why there are more poems about them
than other birds. It is the bird that comes closest to us, and we
can, with Stanley Kunitz, feel some interconnectedness between
animal and human worlds. It would be nice to think that, with
their inquisitive cocked heads and large bright eyes, they knew
something about us. John Freeman considers such questions
philosophically in his 'Gardener's Friend'.

Richard Mabey has written that in the robin we are confronted
by an unafraid, unthreatening being as we rarely are by any other
creature. No wonder we melt, and feel for a moment that we
both live in the same one world, he adds. This is what the poems
illuminate: the Robin in your Brain, says Emily Dickinson.

Hamish Whyte

The Red Robin

Cock Robin, he got a neat tippet in spring,
And he sat in a shed, and heard other birds sing.
And he whistled a ballad as loud as he could,
And built him a nest of oak leaves by the wood,
And finished it just as the celandine pressed
Like a bright burning blaze, by the edge of its nest,
All glittering with sunshine and beautiful rays,
Like high polished brass, or the fire in a blaze;
Then sung a new song on the edge o' the brere;
And so it kept singing the whole of the year.
Till cowslips and wild roses blossomed and died,
The red robin sang by the old spinney side.

John Clare (1793 – 1864)

Robin's Round

I am the proper
Bird for this season –
Not blessed St Turkey,
Born to be eaten.

I'm man's inedible
Permanent bird.
I dine in his garden,
My spoon is his spade.

I'm the true token
Of Christ the Child-King:
I nest in man's stable,
I eat at man's table,
Through all his dark winters
I sing.

UA Fanthorpe (1929 – 2009)

Real life Christmas card

Robin, I watch you. You are perfect robin –
except, shouldn't you be perched on a spade handle?

Robin, you watch me. Am I perfect man – except,
shouldn't I have a trap in my pocket, a gun in my hand?

I, too, am in my winter plumage, not unlike yours,
except, the red is in my breast, not on it.

You sing your robin song, I my man song. They're different,
but they mean the same: winter, territory, greed.

Will we survive, bold eyes, to pick
the seeds in the ground, the seeds in my mind?

The snow man thinks so. Look at his silly smile
slushily spilling down the scarf I gave him.

Norman MacCaig (1910 – 1996)

After Christmas

On New Year's Eve one robin tracked our stride
A good two hundred yards along a hedge
(Or hedge and copse combined, the English way)
Until the path bent through the trees. We lay
Our lunchtime crumbs as end-of-year reward.
Today in woods in Kentish countryside
We saw them, in their scores, ignite inside
Each thicket's heart a ticking pulse of red –
As if there'd been a mantelpiece migration.
We were surprised, almost, on our return,
To find that every silent branch and ledge,
On every card, was still safe-occupied.

Peter Walton

The Key-Note

Where are the songs I used to know,
  Where are the notes I used to sing?
  I have forgotten everything
I used to know so long ago;
Summer has followed after Spring;
  Now Autumn is so shrunk and sere,
I scarcely think a sadder thing
  Can be the Winter of my year.

Yet Robin sings thro' Winter's rest,
  When bushes put their berries on;
  While they their ruddy jewels don,
He sings out of a ruddy breast;
The hips and haws and ruddy breast
  Make one spot warm where snowflakes lie,
They break and cheer the unlovely rest
  Of Winter's pause – and why not I?

Christina Rossetti (1830 – 1894)

To the Robins

Innocent receptacles of my love
which I convey in the form of mealworms
when I can get them, or at other times
disguised as tiny morsels of cheese,

I gaze into your eyes, one at a time,
and you gaze back, trying to predict me,
lurking hopefully on the windowsill
but ready to fly if I turn nasty.

Your love is only for each other.
It is embodied mostly in food;
what you really like is 'courtship feeding' –
beak to beak, as if posing for 'Springwatch'.

When he jumped on you (at this point the pronoun
bifurcates from dual to singular),
my fellow female, he was off in a second.
You quivered with astonishment for minutes.

You definitely preferred the foreplay –
the chocolates and champagne, as it were;
in view of which, accept my platonic
offering: a bowl of little wrigglers.

Fleur Adcock

'I watch the robin'

I watch the robin
whirring at the half
coconut shell hang-
ing from the clothes pole
like a humming bird
it beaks beaks into
the sweet fat and seeds
for its sustenance
and I think of you
hotpenning at your
desk day after day
and the thing I love
is the persistence

Hamish Whyte

'You'll know Her – by Her Foot'

You'll know Her – by Her Foot –
The smallest Gamboge Hand
With Fingers – where the Toes should be –
Would more affront the Sand –

Than this Quaint Creature's Boot –
Adjusted by a Stem –
Without a Button – I could vouch –
Unto a Velvet Limb –

You'll know Her – by Her Vest –
Tight fitting – Orange – Brown –
Inside a Jacket duller –
She wore when she was born –

Her Cap is small – and snug –
Constructed for the Winds –
She'd pass for Barehead – short way off –
But as She Closer stands –

So finer 'tis than Wool –
You cannot feel the Seam –
Nor is it Clasped unto of Band –
Nor held upon – of Brim –

You'll know Her – by Her Voice –
At first – a doubtful Tone –
A sweet endeavor – but as March
To April – hurries on –

She squanders on your Ear
Such Arguments of Pearl –
You beg the Robin in your Brain
To keep the other – still –

Emily Dickinson (1830 – 1886)

Robin Redbreast

It was the dingiest bird
you ever saw, all the color
washed from him, as if
he had been standing in the rain,
friendless and stiff and cold,
since Eden went wrong.
In the house marked For Sale,
where nobody made a sound,
in the room where I lived
with an empty page, I had heard
the squawking of the jays
under the wild persimmons
tormenting him.
So I scooped him up
after they knocked him down,
in league with that ounce of heart
pounding in my palm,
that dumb beak gaping.
Poor thing! Poor foolish life!
without sense enough to stop
running in desperate circles,
needing my lucky help
to toss him back into his element.
But when I held him high,
fear clutched my hand,
for through the hole in his head,
cut whistle-clean …
through the old dried wound
between his eyes
where the hunter's brand
had tunneled out his wits …
I caught the cold flash of the blue
unappeasable sky.

Stanley Kunitz (1905 – 2006)

Gardener's Friend

There's a robin in our garden again,
hopping close whenever we're out there working.
This one's different from the one last year
which increasingly seemed to be trying
to say something urgent as if time was short,
but kept his dignity like a dying prince.
This year's is more artlessly confiding,
like a child putting his hand into yours.
The feathers on his back are ruffled-looking.
He's not so young that he doesn't seem to ask
that aching question the other seemed to ask,
without being able to say what it is,
leaving you with the responsibility
of having a pain brought to you to heal,
just the confiding question and the ache.
All we can do, and we do it separately,
comparing notes afterwards, finding we've each
responded in the same way, is talk to him
as if he understood, reassuringly,
about what's happening and what we're doing.
He hopped up on a dead gooseberry bush
I was digging out and looked at me sideways.
Isn't it a strange thing, I said to him,
pausing from pushing the garden fork in
and levering the stem out by the roots,
to be alive and conscious, and not know why?
He'd helped me see that we had that in common.

John Freeman